W9-BDN-511

20th Century Inventions

DIGITAL REVOLUTION

Stephen Hoare

RSVP
RAINTREE STECK-VAUGHN PUBLISHERS
The Steck-Vaughn Company
Austin, Texas

20th Century Inventions

AIRCRAFT
CARS
COMPUTERS
DIGITAL REVOLUTION
FILM AND TELEVISION
THE INTERNET
LASERS
MEDICAL ADVANCES
NUCLEAR POWER
ROCKETS AND SPACECRAFT
SATELLITES
TELECOMMUNICATIONS

Front cover and title page: A virtual reality simulation

Published by Raintree Steck-Vaughn Publishers,
an imprint of Steck-Vaughn Company

Library of Congress Cataloging-in-Publication Data
Hoare, Stephen.
Digital Revolution / Stephen Hoare.
p. cm.—(20th century inventions)
Includes bibliographical references and index.
Summary: Defines digital technology and demonstrates its applications in the home, workplace, and entertainment, communications, and sound recording industries.
ISBN 0-8172-4897-8
1. Digital electronics—Juvenile literature.
[1. Digital electronics. 2. Electronics.]
I. Title. II. Series.
TK7868.D5H6 1999
621.381—dc21 97-32063

Printed in Italy. Bound in the United States.
1 2 3 4 5 6 7 8 9 0 03 02 01 00 99

Picture acknowledgments
British Telecommunications plc 16 (top); Honeywell 33; Image Bank 8 and 45 (left), 18 (top), 28; Images Colour Library back cover and contents page; Olympus 30 (bottom); Psion 4, 27 (bottom); Science Photo Library/Dr. Jeremy Burgess 12 (bottom)/Michael W. Davidson 6/Charles Falco 5 (bottom)/Gable, Jerrican 20/ George Haling 37/James King-Holmes 43/Damien Lovegrove 14/C.S. Langlois, Publiphoto Diffusion 7/Jerry Mason 24/Peter Menzel 26, 42 and 44 (left)/Hank Morgan 16 (bottom), 40 (bottom)/David Parker 10 (top), 39, 41 (top)/David Parker, Seagate Microelectronics Ltd. 5 (top)/Philippe Platilly, Eurelios 12 (top)/Sittler, Jerrican 38/Wallet, Jerrican 35/Jerome Yeates 23; Sony 13 (bottom), 15 (bottom); Frank Spooner Pictures 40 (top); Tony Stone/Getty 11, 15 (top), 21, 22, 25 (both), 27 (top), 30–31 (top), 34, 41 (bottom); Telegraph Colour Library cover and title page; Wayland Picture Library 9; Zefa Pictures 10 (bottom), 13 (top) and 44 (right), 17 and 45 (right), 18 (bottom), 19, 29, 36. Artwork by Tim Benké.

CONTENTS

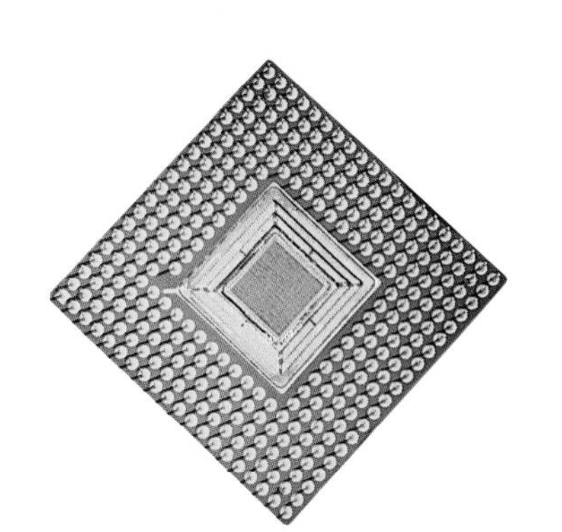

INTRODUCTION

Digital machines like these tiny computers are part of our lives.

Computer technology

The digital revolution is the story of computers. Computer technology is changing all electronic machines and equipment—everything from telephones to video cameras, computer games to hi-fi systems, and washing machines to microwave ovens.

The majority of household and office machines that we use in our daily lives are controlled by microprocessors—miniature computers. Microprocessors may not be able to perform complex calculations, but they are computers because they can be programmed to follow a simple set of tasks.

Early technology

The first computers ran on pulses of electricity conducted through a series of valves—large electrical switches that could send the electrical current along different routes of a circuit. These computers were enormous—the size of a large room—and they were also slow. Today's personal computers (PCs) are much more powerful, and some are small enough to be carried in a briefcase.

To make computers smaller, engineers found a replacement for valves—transistors. Then silicon chips were invented, and these replaced transistors. And now silicon chips are getting smaller and more powerful all the time.

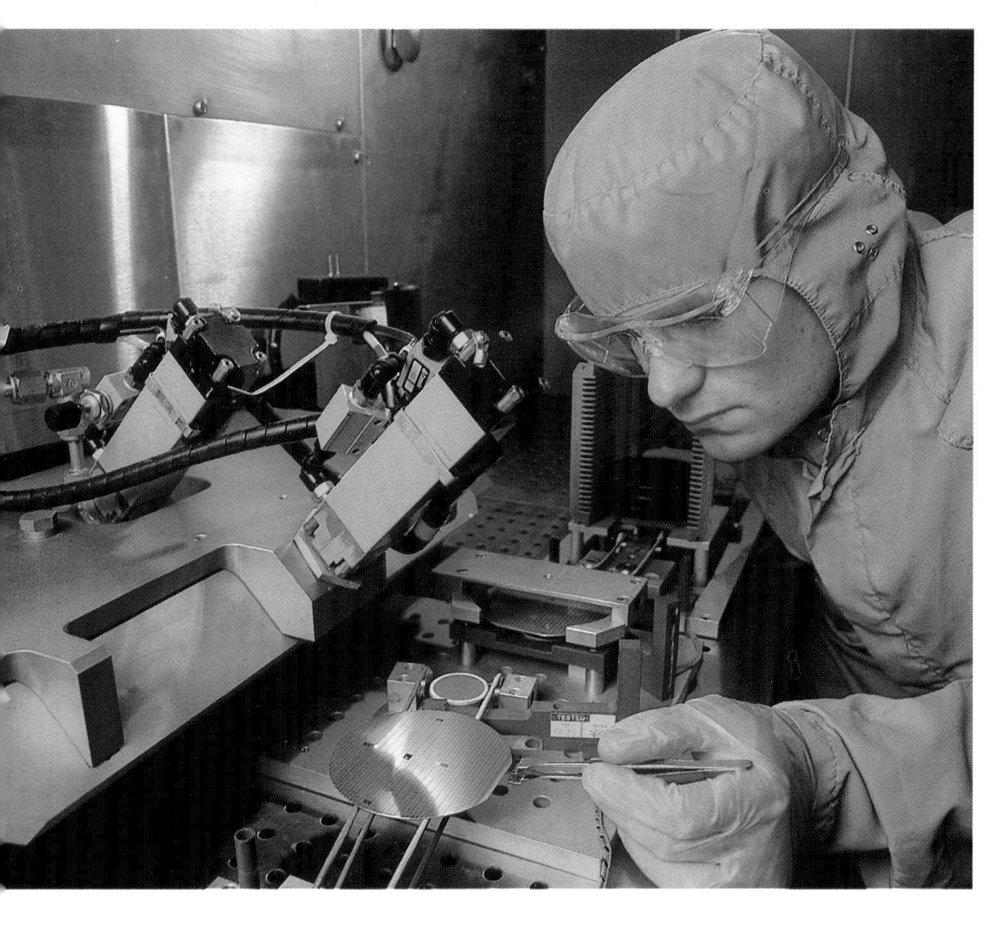

In a dust-free electronic factory, a technician checks that the circuit of a silicon chip has been etched.

Silicon chips

To make silicon chips, crystals of silicon are "grown" in a special oven. The silicon is so pure that it will not conduct electricity until it is treated with certain chemicals. The silicon is cut into very thin wafers.

The circuit is designed and then a detailed drawing is made and reduced photographically. Then it is etched onto the chip in an oven. The chips are then coated in protective plastic. Some silicon chips are so tiny they can fit through the eye of a needle.

In 1959, the American company Texas Instruments created an early version of today's silicon chip, when it etched a circuit with multiple transistors onto a piece of silicon. In 1971, circuit manufacturer Intel reduced all the elements of a computer to fit onto one integrated circuit. Known as "the computer on a chip," Intel's 4004 silicon chip was the size of a baby's fingernail. The world's first microprocessor had been created.

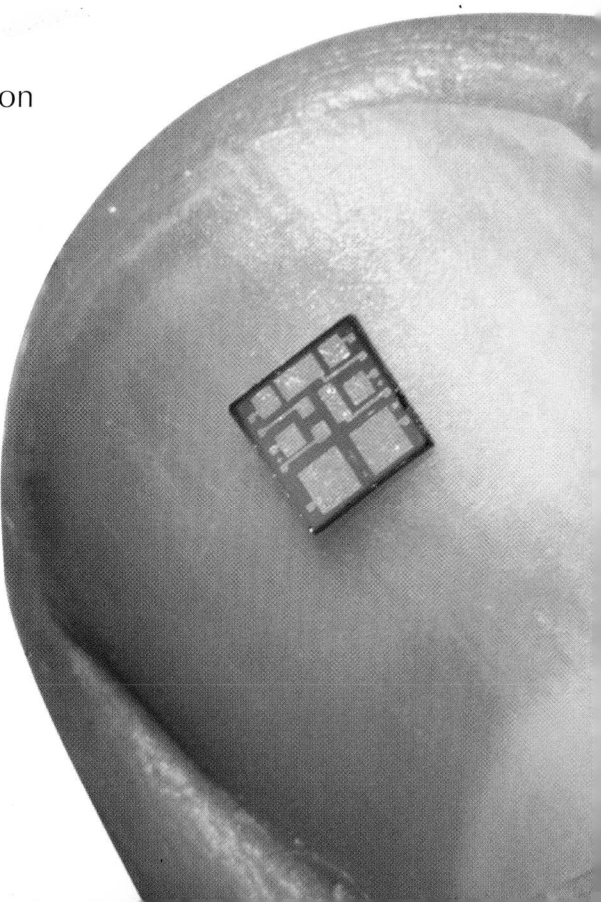

This tiny integrated circuit is small enough to fit onto a fingernail.

WHAT IS DIGITAL TECHNOLOGY?

Intel's first 4004 silicon chip was called a 4-bit chip because it processed data four binary digits at a time. This chip, from one of Intel's Pentium processors, is based on a 64-bit chip, which gives it the power to process information very quickly.

Digital is the language of computers. It is based on a simple number code called binary.

Every number can be expressed as a binary code. In binary, 0 is 0000, 1 is 0001, 2 is 0010, 3 is 0011, and so on. Binary code is similar to smoke signals or Morse Code, where information is translated into puffs of smoke or dots and dashes.

Computers and microprocessors work on binary code, which acts as an electrical switch, where 1 switches on the current and 0 switches it off. When you use binary, you are storing numbers or digits of information.

Developed through computers, digital technology is now being applied to almost every sort of electronic machine. The rapid advances in digital technology are bringing together other technologies, such as television, radio, telecommunications, and computers. Music, sound, and images are now recorded and transmitted in digital code to improve on the quality of information and increase the quantity that can be stored.

Analog

An analog is a copy. In sound recording, for example, the grooves in a vinyl record cause the needle of a record player to vibrate, reproducing a copy of the original sound.

Before digital recording, sound and images were recorded and converted into electrical pulses or radio waves, which could then be converted back into sounds and images. Some of the original quality was lost at every stage of the process. However, by converting sound or pictures into digital code, the quality can be reproduced perfectly.

A technician works at the mixing desk of a digital sound studio. He overlays separately recorded tracks of backing vocals and instruments to create a final recording.

Quality

Anything can be stored and reproduced as digital information: not just numbers but words, pictures, and sound. Digital is an exact representation of the sound or image in binary code. This never changes, so digital recording means that the sound or pictures can be broadcast or reproduced at their original quality every time.

True digital quality of fine sound and picture details requires a large amount of binary information to be recorded. To do this, greater bandwidth—space for storing electronic data—is required. Audiotapes are thin and have a narrow bandwidth. Videotapes contain sound and moving pictures and need to contain a lot more information, so they have a broad bandwidth. Compact discs (CDs) have broad bandwidths compared with the vinyl records that they have replaced.

COMPACT DISCS

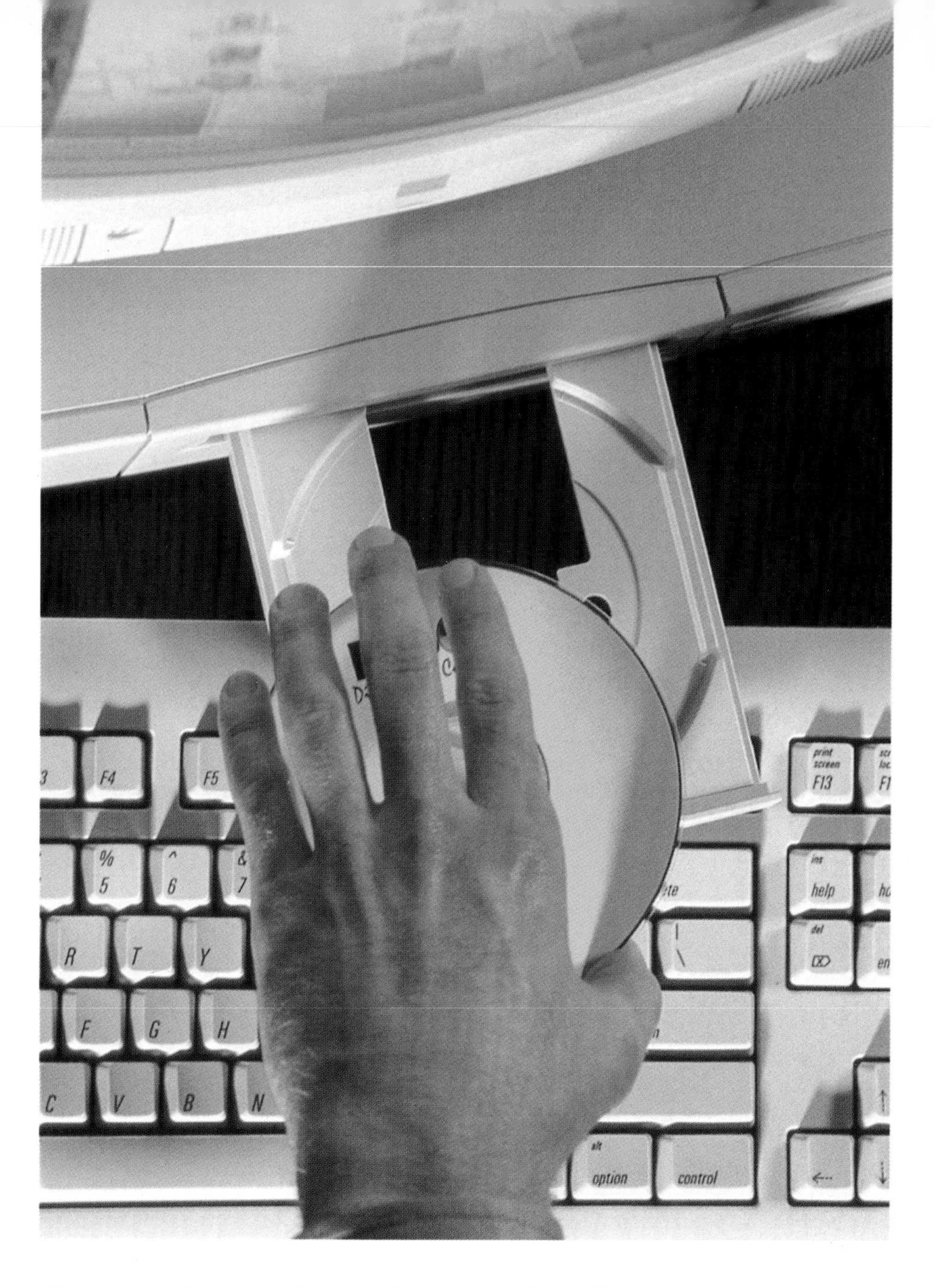

Software on a CD-ROM is loaded onto a PC, to be stored in the computer's memory.

Compact discs can be used to store digitally recorded sounds, words, and images and can play them back as music, photographs, multimedia "books," videos, or computer games.

Digital technology was first applied to audio recording. Digital recording onto CDs transformed sound quality. Since then, CDs have been developed that will store video, photographs, interactive games, and multimedia.

CDs can now be used across a range of machines. Many computers can play audio CDs, while interactive games CDs can be used with either a television or a computer screen.

CD-ROMs for education

CD-ROMs are ideal for interactive learning. Working alone, pupils can study at their own pace. Following on-screen instructions, educational programs guide the user through a series of topics, and students can answer questions with multimedia text and pictures. Many schools and colleges have access to recording studios and are able to produce their own multimedia CD-ROMs, containing examples of students' writing, taped interviews, photographs, videos, and artwork.

CDs are helping different technologies come together. Multimedia CD-ROMs can combine text, sound, still pictures, animation, and video clips.

Videotapes can now be made digitally, and the new digital video CDs, called DVDs, can store long films, which can be viewed on a television screen through a special player. You can even buy a CD recorder that will digitally record your voice.

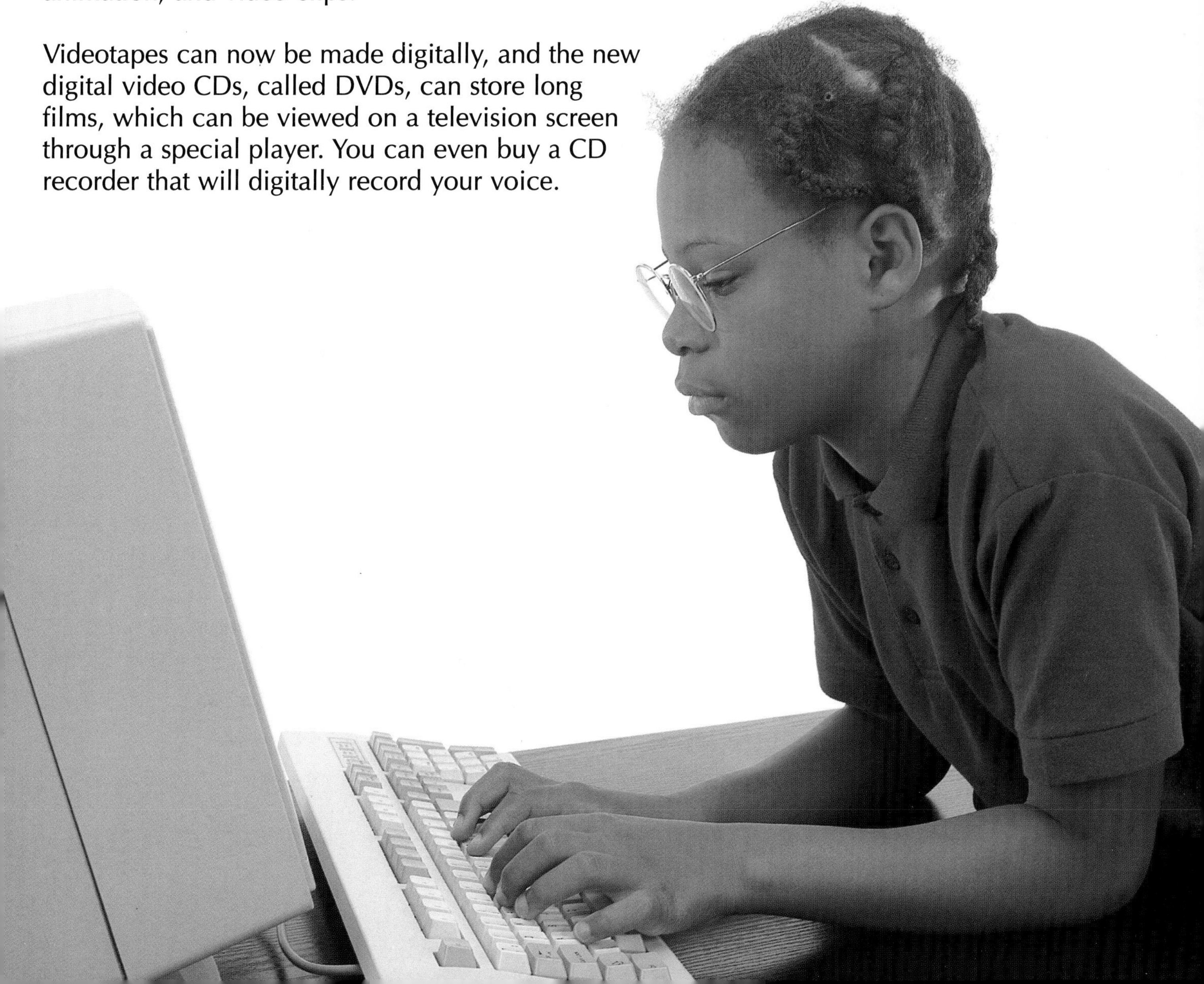

You can change the software on your computer by loading it with a CD containing new operating instructions.

CHANNELS OF COMMUNICATION

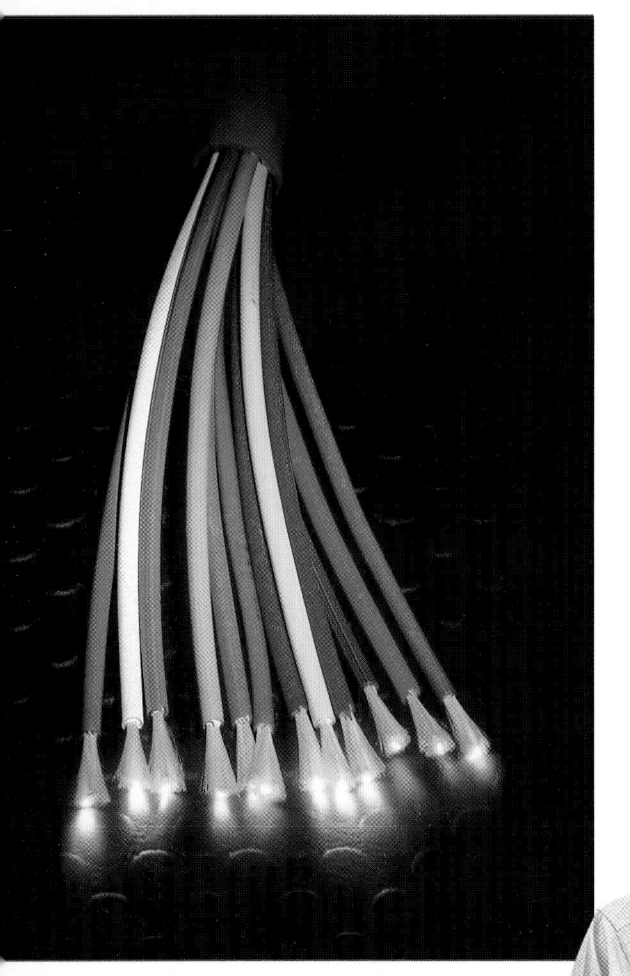

Glass fibers in these fiberoptic cables are as light, flexible, and fine as human hair. Pulses of laser light travel along these fibers and transmit sound, data, and images through long-distance cable networks.

The telephone was invented 150 years ago, and the world now has 900 million telephone lines, but over the next few years the number of telephone lines is likely to double. This is because more and more lines are needed to cope with the ever-increasing amount of digital communication that is taking place all over the globe.

Copper telephone wire can transmit sound as well as a limited amount of digital information—data—in the form of facsimiles (faxes) and electronic mail (E-mail). But some new telephone lines will make use of fiberoptic cables, which can transmit millions of bits of information at the same time. Fiberoptic cables are capable of carrying telephone conversations, computer data, and video pictures.

Letters and documents are often sent by fax rather than by mail. As instant as a phone call, text, diagrams, and photographs are sent from one fax machine to another via a telephone line.

Modern mobile telephones are light, compact, and easy to use. Small enough to fit into a pocket, mobile telephones can store hundreds of names and telephone numbers and take messages when the telephone is switched off.

Telephones

Mobile telephones can transmit data all over the world. The mobile telephones of the future will act as handheld computers and could even transmit video pictures. The most modern mobile telephones already have large memories, keyboards, and visual displays and are capable of word-processing, storing information, producing spreadsheets, and sending faxes. Soon, people will be able to buy a powerful computer that is also a television, video, stereo, and telephone all rolled into one.

The Internet

The Internet, or "Net," is a vast network of millions of computers all over the world linked by telephone lines and cables. The Internet allows people to communicate with each other and to access huge amounts of information.

ENTERTAINMENT

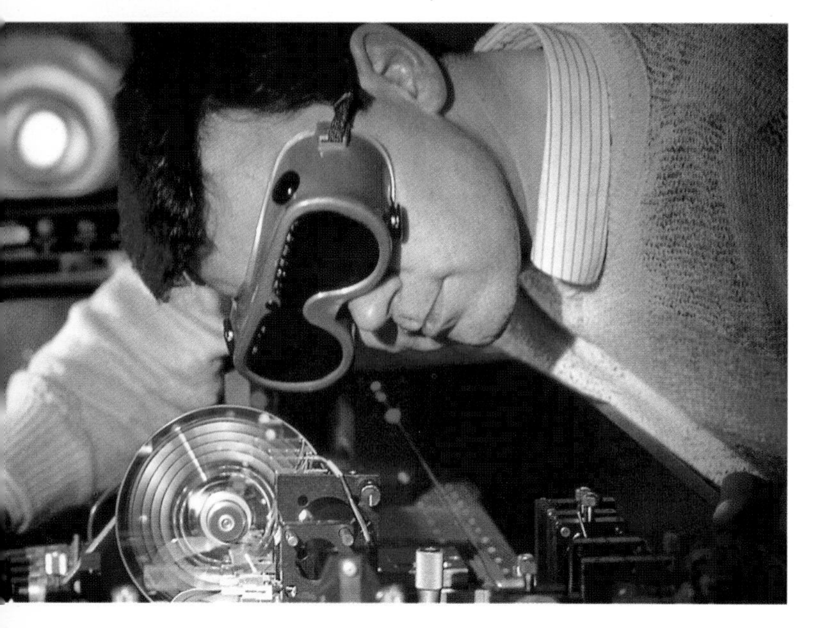

A researcher checks the position of a master CD, which is about to be etched by laser.

Compact discs

Developed in 1979 by the Japanese electronics manufacturer Sony and the Dutch company Philips, CDs are a way of storing digital information. The first CDs were used for audio recording.

CDs are made by feeding digital data to a laser, which produces millions of tiny marks, called "pits," on a glass master disc. The spaces between the pits are bumps, called "lands," which are also an important part of the recording. Together, the pits and lands make up the on-off signals for binary code.

A metal imprint of the glass master disc is used as a mold for producing large numbers of CDs from very thin aluminum. The discs are covered with a protective coating. The pits and lands on a CD are "read" by a laser and converted back into digital signals, which can be translated into sound by a CD player.

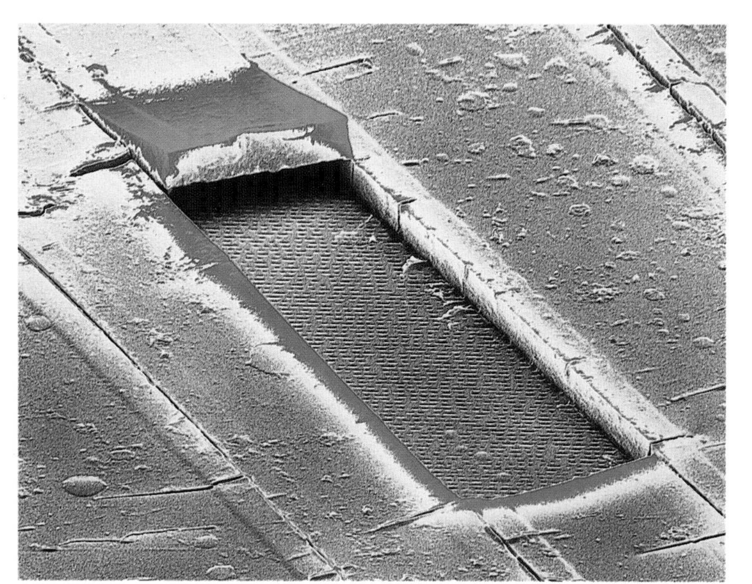

The surface of a CD is made up of millions of pits and lands, which contain the digital information to create a perfect recording.

Personal stereos

In the late 1970s, the head of Sony, Akio Morita, developed an idea for a personal stereo—a small stereo cassette player that could be listened to through headphones and carried in a pouch slung from the shoulder. The first personal stereo, the Sony Walkman, went on sale in 1979. Today, personal stereos can play CDs. The Sony CD-ROM Discman allows users to listen to their favorite CDs and even output them to a computer.

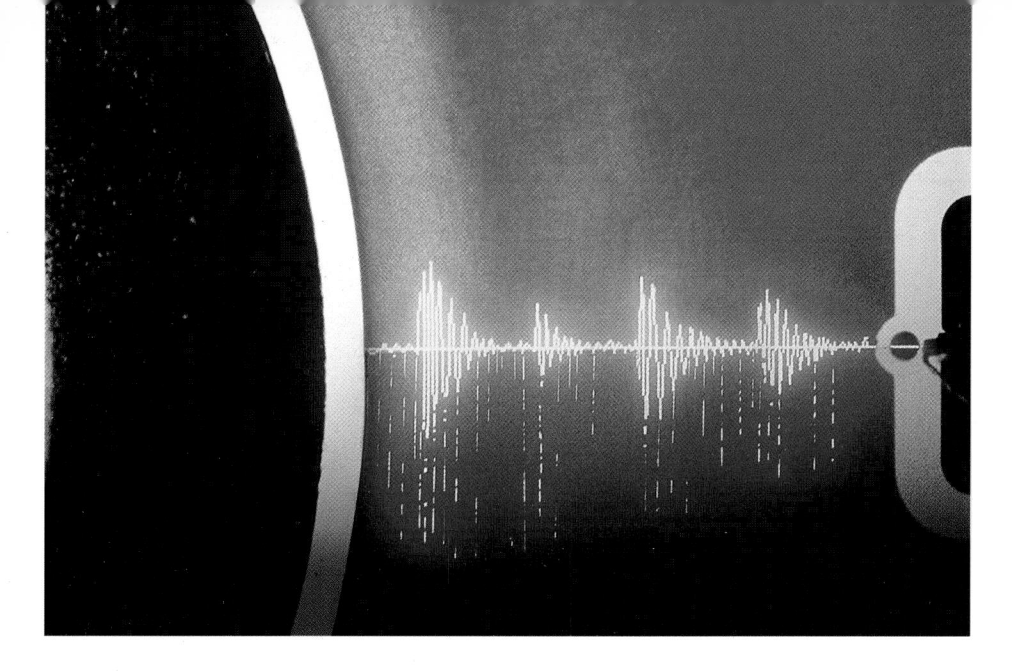

A beam of laser light is reflected by the etched surface of a CD to reproduce perfect sound quality.

CD-Midi

In 1989, the Japanese company JVC introduced a new type of CD, which could control electronic musical instruments like synthesizers and rhythm boxes. The discs contain pre-programmed music, and when inserted into a special player called a CD-Midi, they will play back the music on the synthesizer, allowing the user to alter the way the music sounds.

Music on computer

Multimedia computers and Apple Macintosh computers can record and play back sound. Now, engineers are busy designing a computer that will play and create music—changing the rhythm and speed. Musicians will be able to use a special keyboard that interfaces, or communicates, with the computer.

Recording

Marketed for the first time in the late 1980s, digital audiotape (DAT) enables people to make CD-quality recordings on special cassettes. This can also be done using the more recently developed digital compact cassette (DCC), a digital recording device that can be used with ordinary audiocassettes. Manufacturers now produce a mini-CD recorder so that people can make their own recordings on a CD at home.

The Sony Walkman was the first personal stereo.

MULTIMEDIA

Digital technology has created multimedia—recording words, sound, and pictures in digital code, which can be etched onto CDs and read by a laser.

Multimedia is computer technology that combines sound, still and moving images, and text. It allows CDs to be played on a computer, a television, or a stereo system. Multimedia players plug directly into these machines to provide high-quality graphics and sound, whereas multimedia CD-ROMs can be loaded into a computer and "read" like a book.

Multimedia has opened up a world of music, games, and information that is proving very popular with children. This boy is using a multimedia CD-ROM to learn a foreign language.

Above **These girls are using a handheld game machine.**

Audio CDs are simply high-quality sound recordings, but multimedia CD-ROMs and interactive game CDs are controllable. When the disc is loaded onto a computer, the person can then "read" the CD-ROM on the computer screen, choosing from a range of options.

CD-ROM reference "books" contain a blend of images, video clips, still pictures, and sound. Choosing options from a menu enables the reader to find and select information. The pages of information stored on disc can also be printed out.

Games

With an interactive program and 3-D images, the player of a game CD feels almost part of the action. Moving a joystick changes the screen image, allowing the player to control the game's cartoon animation and speed. Some games can be played by several players in their own living rooms or from different places through telephone lines.

Right **Sony's game machine, *Yaroze*, which allows players to write their own programs for computer games by combining 3-D images, sound, and animation**

HOME VISION

A television studio picks up satellite pictures from the other side of the world.

Digital broadcasts use broadband communications such as cable or satellite to transmit high-quality images. Because a greater amount of data can be compressed in digital format over a broadband network, many more television channels can be transmitted at the same time, giving viewers a greater choice. Digital satellite transmission will mean that up to 200 television channels can be beamed to television sets all over the world.

Engineers are developing television sets that will improve home viewing. Screens are now wider and completely flat to give picture quality like that in movie theaters. Some wide-screen television sets have stereo digital sound quality.

Digital picture processing is available on some television sets, which enables them to receive digital television broadcasts as well as to play the new digital videodiscs (DVDs). This technology is called high-definition television (HDTV). HDTV makes it possible to have much larger wide-screen televisions without losing picture quality.

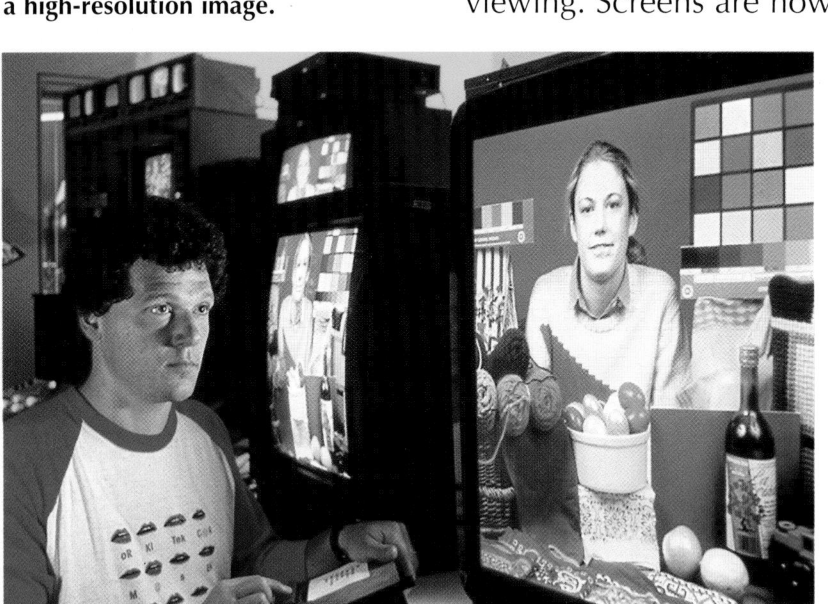

A scientist demonstrates high-definition television, also known as HDTV. The screen is composed of as many as 2,000 lines, giving a high-resolution image.

In normal, nondigital television broadcasts, the pictures are derived from a signal, which is broken down into horizontal lines. The more lines there are, the better the picture quality. In the United States and Japan, televisions have 525 lines, and in the United Kingdom there are 625 lines. HDTV increases these numbers of line resolution up to 2,000.

Digital videodiscs

The digital videodisc was developed in 1987 by Sony and Philips. It is a large-format CD, which can be played back through a DVD player on an analog or a digital television set. A DVD can be searched and replayed exactly like a videotape, but has much better picture quality and a digital stereo sound track.

The compact videodisc can store a massive amount of digital information—enabling a full feature-length film to be replayed with stereo sound and high-definition picture quality.

Unlike audio CDs, the DVD is double-sided—two CDs are glued back-to-back and the discs are double layered. This means that on each side there are two separate layers of readable information, one below the other. To read the layer underneath, the laser changes focus slightly and shines through the transparent outer layer. A double-sided 8.5 gigabyte DVD plays for a maximum of two hours and can hold seven times more material than a standard CD.

Just as there are CDs and CD-ROMs, one day in the near future a DVD-ROM and an interactive digital videodisc (DVD-I) will be developed. These inventions will lead to the creation of new types of films, games, and multimedia programs.

COMMUNICATIONS

Cable and satellite

Satellites several thousand miles above the earth receive radio waves from transmitters on Earth and beam them back over a large area of the earth's surface. Satellite signals are now so powerful that they can be picked up by a small dish television aerial on the side of a house.

Cable television is transmitted to homes through fiberoptic cables that are laid under the ground. Fiberoptic cable is made of glass fiber so pure that you could see through a sheet 60 mi. (100 km) thick. It can carry 2.5 gigabytes per second—250,000 times more than twisted copper cable.

Above **High above the earth, a communications satellite receives radio signals from a broadcast station on Earth and beams them across vast areas.**

Subscribers to satellite or cable television need a card reader—an electronic black box that unscrambles the digital signal. A smart card with a microchip is inserted into the card reader.

Telephones

Sound, data, images, and video pictures can all be sent down a telephone line. Digital telephone lines have a higher bandwidth and can transmit data 30 times faster than a conventional analog telephone line.

Digital broadcasts

Converting images and sound into computer code enables data to be compressed. Cameras and broadcast transmitters are changing to digital code.

Right **Set to receive signals from satellites, dish antennas beam digital television broadcasts into the home.**

Huge dishes like this one receive satellite signals and broadcast them to viewers.

Digital radio broadcasting (DRB) has been launched in Great Britain and in the United States as cable FM. It offers sound quality as good as that of a CD. To listen to digital radio, people will need to replace their old radios with new equipment. To watch digital television, people will have to buy equipment that will allow their televisions to "read" the digital signals.

Digital television offers many more channels to watch. Ten digital television channels can be squeezed into the same frequency needed to broadcast just one analog channel.

Interactive television

In the United States, Time Warner Cable's Full Service Network in Orlando, Florida, offers video, interactive games, and home shopping on demand. The subscriber uses a keypad to choose options from the television screen.These are then fed back to the television company's file server—a powerful computer that can store and play a vast library of films and programs on CD.

Once the video, game, or service is selected, it is compressed into digital pulses of laser light and transmitted along a fiberoptic cable to a node (junction) near the subscriber's home. At the node, the digital light signal is converted into a radio signal and sent on the last stage of its journey, via a cable, to the subscriber's home. There it is converted into a television signal by an electronic box on top of the television set.

THE INTERNET

Some cafés offer customers the chance to gain access to the Internet over a cup of coffee or cool drink.

The Internet is a communications network that links computers across the globe. The network is shared by more than 40 million people.

The system is based on a former U.S. military computer network called the ARPANET. It was originally set up to keep communications from being wiped out in the event of a nuclear war. By transmitting digital information via international telephone lines, data could be sent from one computer to another.

To access the Internet, you need a service provider that can give you the correct connections and programs to help you find your way around the Internet.

The Internet enables people to send E-mail to other computer users all over the world. To send somebody an E-mail, you type a message on your computer, enter the other person's E-mail address, and press the "send" key. The message is transmitted down a telephone line in seconds. E-mail can also be used to send files or data from your computer, including text, pictures, or even sound. In this way, computer users can share information, news, and ideas.

The World Wide Web

On the World Wide Web are pages of information and images called Web sites, which can be viewed by Internet users. Using a navigation program supplied by the service provider, people can browse among thousands of Web sites, using key words to search for information they need.

Web sites hold a massive amount of information, much of it in multimedia form, stored by governments, businesses, educational establishments, and other organizations.

Using the Internet, people can transfer information and pictures from a Web site onto their own computer, where they can store and print out the information.

Schools can gain access to educational Web sites offering material specially written and selected for educational use.

The modem

To access the Internet and to send E-mail, you need a modulator demodulator (modem). First used in the 1950s, the modem is like a translator, which allows computers to speak to each other over the telephone line.

The modem converts digital data used by computers into an analog audio signal, which can be sent down the telephone line. Digital code enables electronic data to be transmitted at very high speed, compressing a vast amount of information into a series of high-frequency pulses or signals. This makes it possible to send words and pictures down telephone lines digitally in large quantities and at great speed.

MOBILE COMMUNICATIONS

The mobile telephone is a useful tool for busy people on the move. Many people such as doctors, teachers, and social workers use mobile telephones to keep in touch.

Mobile telephones have been available since the mid-1980s. Run on batteries, mobile telephones operate without telephone wires, so they can be carried around and used at any time.

Small and compact, a mobile telephone has an earpiece, a mouthpiece, a keypad, and a display that can show short text messages. This allows you to see the number you are dialing or to call numbers programmed into the telephone's memory chip.

Cellular networks

Mobile telephones have small aerials, which transmit telephone calls as radio signals. Mobile telephone signals are picked up by base stations—aerials sited on top of tall buildings or hills. Base stations receive calls and re-transmit them to their destination—whether that is another mobile telephone or an ordinary telephone.

Transmitting over a limited range of around 50 mi. (80 km), each base station's area of communication is called a cell. A mobile telephone's cellular network is made up of lots of overlapping cells, and mobile telephones are sometimes known as cell phones.

As you travel, your telephone picks up the strongest signal. But there are places where a mobile telephone cannot receive a signal, for example, in mountainous areas, in deep forests, or in tunnels or in underground parking lots.

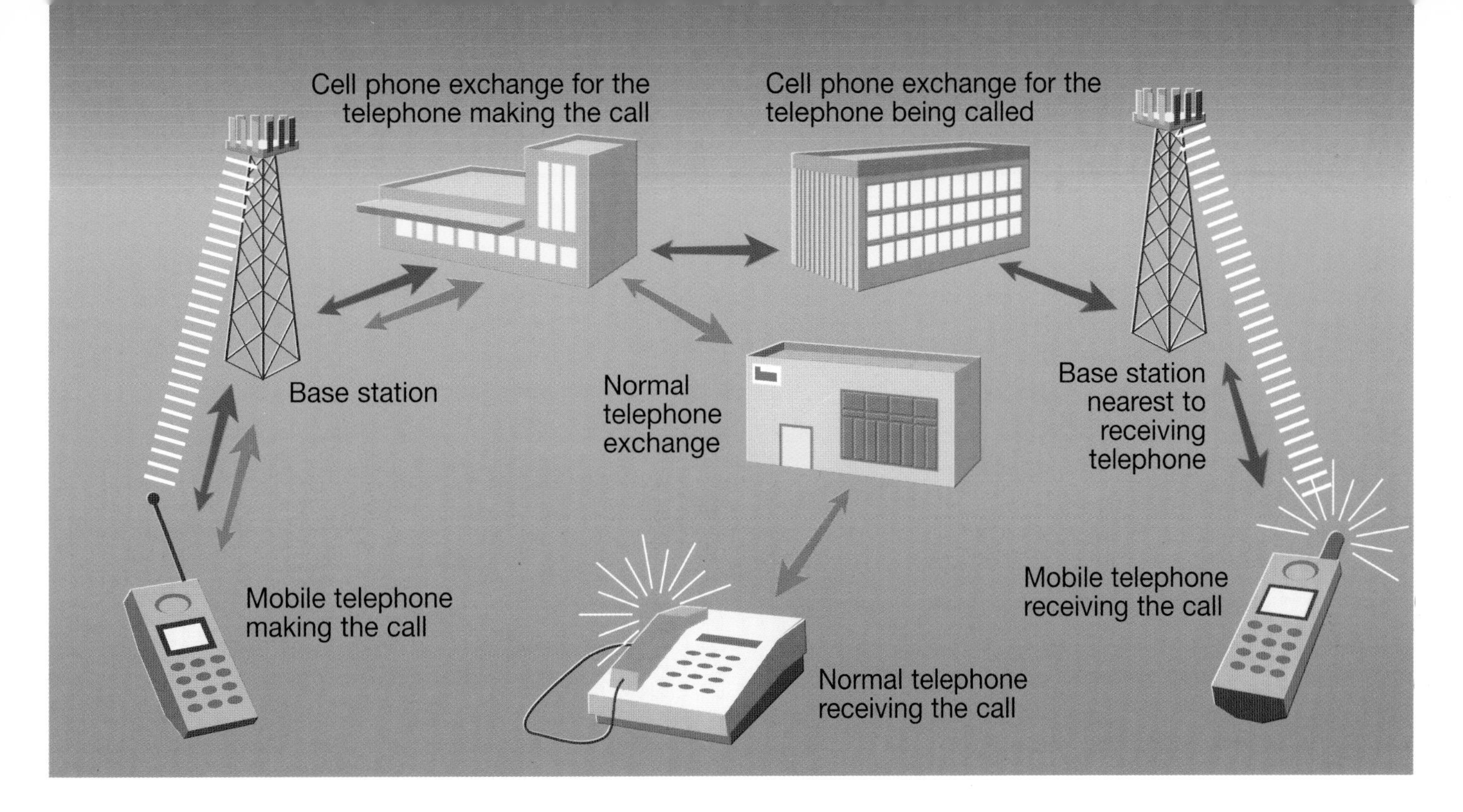

A cellular telephone network. Base stations or transmitters create a network of cells that route mobile telephone calls across the country.

Analog or digital?

There are two types of networks for mobile telephones—analog and digital. Digital networks compress data and can deal with more calls than analog ones. This means that the telephone signal is clearer and there is almost no chance of being cut off. Digital telephones also provide greater security, because people cannot listen to other people's calls by using a scanner.

Digital networks are also called GSM, which stands for "global system for mobile communications." This means that you can use your digital telephone almost anywhere in the world, and some GSM telephones use satellite communications to transmit signals around the world.

Digital telephones have a subscriber identity module (SIM) card (also called a smart card), which is the size of a plastic credit card. The card contains a microchip that gives access to the network. If you take your SIM card out of your mobile telephone and fit it into another compatible telephone, the calls you make will be charged to your account.

For extra security, some telephones can be programmed with a personal identity number (PIN), which will keep other people from using your telephone without your permission.

A GSM mobile telephone and smart card. A smart card is like having your own portable phone number. Individuals can use a smart card in any GSM phone anywhere in the world and have calls charged to their account.

THE DIGITAL WORKPLACE

The electronic home office

With a PC, fax machine, mobile telephone, E-mail, and the Internet at home, who needs to work in an office? Because powerful machines like these are readily available, instant communication means that more people are working from home. Working at home and using computers is called telecommuting and is a trend that is likely to increase in the future. In the United States in 1996, there were more than 8 million telecommuters.

The complete home office. In addition to the computer screen and keyboard, the telecommuter has a telephone link, a modem for transmitting data from one computer to another, and a CD-ROM drive that accepts new software.

Even in offices, people often send each other messages and information by E-mail. Faxes and E-mail reduce the need for face-to-face meetings, but when groups of people do need to get together to talk, they do not have to meet in person; they can use a system called videoconferencing (see pages 28–29).

Many creative people like writers and designers already work from home, but modern telecommunications and computers allow other workers to do the same. Teachers and lecturers can even check their students' work via a computer link.

Freedom

Working at home enables people to organize their work to suit their lifestyles and to decide when and for how long they work. For example, telecommuting can be an advantage for a parent who needs to work flexible hours to fit in with taking care of children.

Left **Rush-hour traffic jams and congested city centers are helping make telecommuting a more attractive alternative to the daily problem of getting to work.**

Telecommuting means that, in the future, people will no longer have to live near their place of work or travel long distances to get to the office. They can live anywhere they like, as long as there is a telephone line with a digital exchange or a cable network that will allow them to transfer computer data.

Mobile offices

People who have to travel a great deal can now take their offices with them, thanks to mobile telephones and to transferable telephone numbers that can switch the caller to whichever telephone the person happens to be using at the time.

Mobile telephones can store incoming messages and display them on a display panel. They can send and receive short faxes and E-mail and can be connected to a computer. Linked to a laptop computer via a tiny modem, a mobile telephone will even allow the user to access the Internet.

Right **This businessman opens his laptop computer to create an "outdoor office." With almost as much power as a desktop PC, laptops are used by people whose work involves traveling.**

By linking microchips together, engineers built personal computers—computers that did not need armies of technicians feeding in instructions but would, instead, run on specially written software. As microchips became more complex, PCs quickly grew to become as powerful as the huge old computers yet cheap and small enough for people to buy to use in the office or in the home.

Bill Gates, the head of Microsoft, is now one of the richest men in the world, thanks to the huge success of MS-DOS and Windows.

Home computers

In 1976, Apple made the first computer designed especially for people to buy and use at home. The computer's built-in keyboard, sound, color, and graphics made it simple to use. IBM launched its PC in 1981, using software supplied by a then-small company called Microsoft.

Microsoft's software was called Microsoft Disk Operating System (MS-DOS), and this was joined by Windows—one of the simplest and most useful programs for nonexperts to use. Today, Microsoft is one of the most powerful companies in the world.

As technology has advanced, computers have become cheaper as well as faster and more efficient. This is because of the number and complexity of microchips and the vastly increased capacity of random access memory (RAM). RAM is the memory of the computer, which holds the data the computer is using while it is switched on. The RAM is cleared every time the computer is turned off. The more RAM the computer has, the faster and more efficiently it can work.

Because they are small and light, laptop computers can be used anywhere.

Portable computers

Computers are getting smaller! The palmtop is like an entire office that fits on the palm of your hand. It is a pocket-sized computer with a tough carrying case that opens to reveal a keyboard and a screen. A palmtop computer can store data in its memory, so many people use them as diary, address book, and personal organizer. Some palmtops even have built-in digital sound recorders that store verbal messages.

But the real value of the palmtop is that it can be connected with a cable to powerful office machines such as desktop PCs, modems, printers, and mobile telephones. Some palmtops also have tiny transmitters that allow them to send data to other computers or palmtops without the need for a cable.

With standard software, palmtops can be used as word processors or to create databases that can be printed out.

Who needs a PC when you can download software from the Internet without one? A tiny computer, the *JavaStation,* was launched by Sun Microsystems and Morse Computers in 1997. It connects to your television and allows you to obtain information and games from the Internet.

A palmtop computer connected to a desktop PC

VIDEOCONFERENCING

Videoconferencing enables executives in big companies to hold meetings or conferences via a computer screen. By networking (linking) their computers over a broadband communications channel, such as fiberoptic cable, a group of up to 50 people can see and hear one another even though they are based in different locations around the country—or even the world.

Using Windows-based software, videoconferencing transmits two-way sound and moving images in "real time" (as they happen). As someone speaks, his or her voice is transmitted and a digital closed-circuit television (CCTV) camera on top of the PC captures moving pictures and presents them on a panel on the computer screen.

A tiny CCTV camera, a microphone, and a cable link enable this woman to use her computer to hold a "meeting" with colleagues.

Videoconferencing is often used by international companies to allow people from around the world to hold important business meetings.

Useful applications

Videoconferencing is already used by some universities to teach students in their homes and, in the future, children could be taught at home via computer. This technology would be especially useful for schools in isolated rural communities. Teachers of some subjects would teach large groups of pupils at once, rather than traveling among schools to teach the same lesson to many small groups.

Videoconferencing could also make it easier for people to buy things by using their computer screen because they could "meet" and talk to a salesperson. The system could also be used for home banking and other business transactions.

ELECTRONICS IN THE HOME

Many everyday household machines are now controlled or programmed digitally through inbuilt microprocessors that tell the machine what to do.

Modern refrigerators have a microchip that allows the refrigerator to keep a constant temperature and save energy by switching the motor on or off to control the temperature.

Ovens also have microprocessors that control the heat and operate a timer to switch the oven on or off. The microprocessors in washing machines control the complex programs for different wash cycles. These set the time and temperature of the wash and the timing of rinse and spin stages.

Above **The modern home is full of electronic gadgets.**

Heating and lighting

Digital microprocessors are now built into central heating and hot water control panels, and a control computer can collect information about how much energy your home is using. Homes of the future will have a computer that can help the owner program the controls to heat and light the house, using as little fuel as possible. Sensors could be used to set lighting to switch on or off at set times and to gradually increase artificial lighting as it gets dark at night.

Watches and cameras

A digital watch is not just one that shows the time and date on a display. It is controlled by a tiny computer chip. A fully automatic digital watch has a program that works out the day and the month from any set starting time. A digital watch can also make more complicated adjustments, such as allowing for the extra day in a leap year.

The digital camera does not take pictures on film. Instead, it stores digital information in a computer memory, which it can download electronically when it is plugged into a multimedia computer. Once loaded onto the computer's memory, the images can be altered with special software. The picture can be printed, either on its own or as part of a document. The images can be seen magnified on a computer screen.

The digital camera works by breaking down an image into pixels—thousands of tiny dots of color in a grid pattern. These are coded and stored by the computer.

Left **A small screen at the back of this digital camera displays the image. The camera is connected to a special printer, which is printing out the photograph.**

COMMUNICATING MACHINES

Digital technology allows machines that contain microprocessors to talk to each other and to act "intelligently."

The intelligent home of the future might contain a refrigerator that automatically uses a telephone line to re-order food from the local supermarket. Imagine a wall-mounted notepad that would display messages that have come in over the telephone or the Internet while you were out. Imagine a security system with a sensor that would automatically switch on the heating if there were people at home outside the pre-programmed hours.

This diagram shows how cables connecting home appliances could allow them to "talk" with each other and to respond to controls from a central control panel.

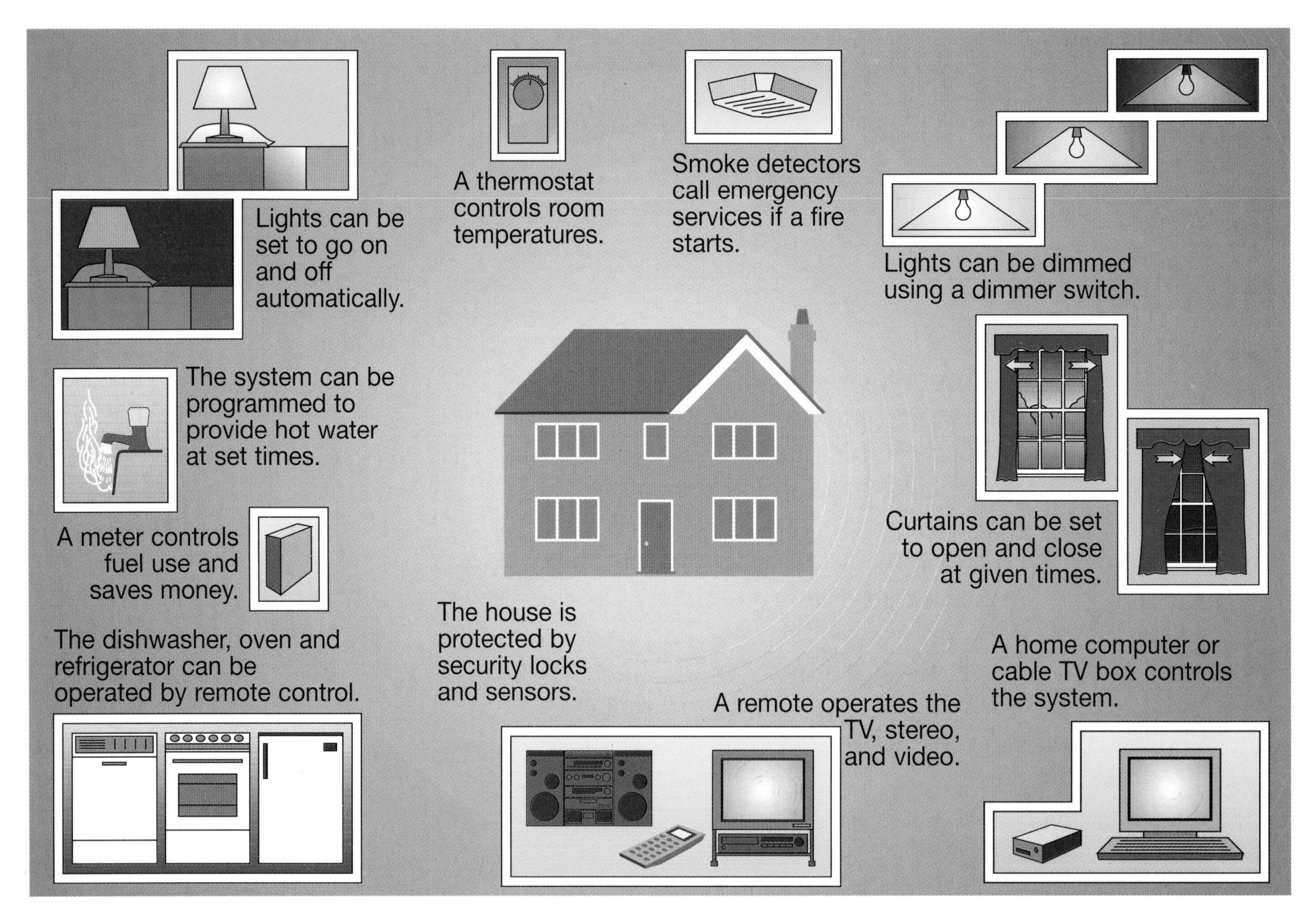

The digital signals that would control these machines could be sent down electric power circuits and received through specially adapted plugs. Or machines could be connected by an internal cable network feeding into a computer.

A digital, wall-mounted unit controls a household's heating system and saves money on fuel bills.

Self-reading meters

It is now possible to have a meter that tells you how much gas, electricity, or water you are using. Linked with the supply company's office through a modem, the meter can send and receive data, enabling the supply company to send you a bill automatically. This system is called digital remote metering.

Digital remote metering could help reduce household bills by telling householders when energy costs are cheapest and when they should use their household appliances. It could also show them which household appliance is costing the most to run.

Energy-saving homes

Intelligent systems can minimize the use of energy. Some experimental houses show that good design and modern technology can save energy and help reduce the amount of air pollution.

Digital technology can help coordinate household heating systems. A digital heating controller can adapt the temperature setting on the boiler to the temperature of the house. Battery-powered digital sensors on radiators adjust the heat output and a sensitive control system could allow solar panels to be used alongside conventional central heating.

HOME SECURITY

An increasing number of homes are now being fitted with sophisticated security devices such as passive infrared (PIR) intruder alarms and CCTV entry telephones. First developed for industry, these electronic devices are now becoming less expensive, and many systems have been adapted for the home market.

Alarms

Most home systems use PIR movement detectors, in which an alarm is triggered if a beam of invisible light is broken.

Basic alarm systems ring a loud bell if they are triggered, but recently developed alarms linked to digital still or video cameras can do some amazing things. If a fire or an intruder alarm is activated, the alarm system's control panel will automatically dial an alarm message and transmit digital pictures via a modem to a security control center. Watching on a television monitor screen, the security officer calls the police or the fire department.

Entry telephones linked to a CCTV camera and keypad security codes make houses more secure than ever before.

This room in a computerized house has a range of home entertainment equipment. A computer controls all the household systems, including lighting, heating, and security.

Closed-circuit TV

Some houses and apartment buildings are now protected by CCTV. A miniature CCTV camera is positioned near a door and will start recording when someone presses the doorbell. The CCTV camera transmits pictures that can be seen by selecting a spare channel on the television set.

Digital CCTV produces clearer images than ordinary CCTV. By making automatic adjustments for light and improving the image, the camera can produce good-quality images, even in poor light.

Sometimes, CCTV links to a monitoring station where security officers watch panels of screens and check for intruders.

Automated homes

In the United States, some luxury homes are automated—controlled by machines that automatically do certain things. A central control panel programs the household gadgets and services even if the owner is away from home. Using a special code, a homeowner can dial home from a mobile telephone and switch on the oven to cook dinner. By tapping in another code, the owner could open the driveway gates or the garage doors or turn on the house lights and close the curtains.

An automated home might also include a home entertainment system—a central stereo system that plays music in each room. The music can be adjusted or turned on or off, using a keypad in each room.

CARS

On-board computers

On-board electronics are taking a lot of the strain out of driving. Special computers inside the car give the driver information about the car's performance and the amount of fuel it is using. They also give early warning of mechanical problems.

Motor racing

Formula One Grand Prix Racing is a fiercely competitive sport. Driving a Formula One car demands great skill and courage, but a computer can also help to win races. Under the hood of most modern racing cars lies a very powerful engine and a tiny but equally powerful computer. The computer monitors the car's performance—recording information such as speed and fuel consumption. Racing cars made by the Lotus Company have a system where information from the car's computer can be picked up by an aerial in the driver's helmet. The driver sees the data on a tiny screen mounted inside the crash helmet.

This Formula One racing car uses a complex computer to analyze performance and to give early warning of problems.

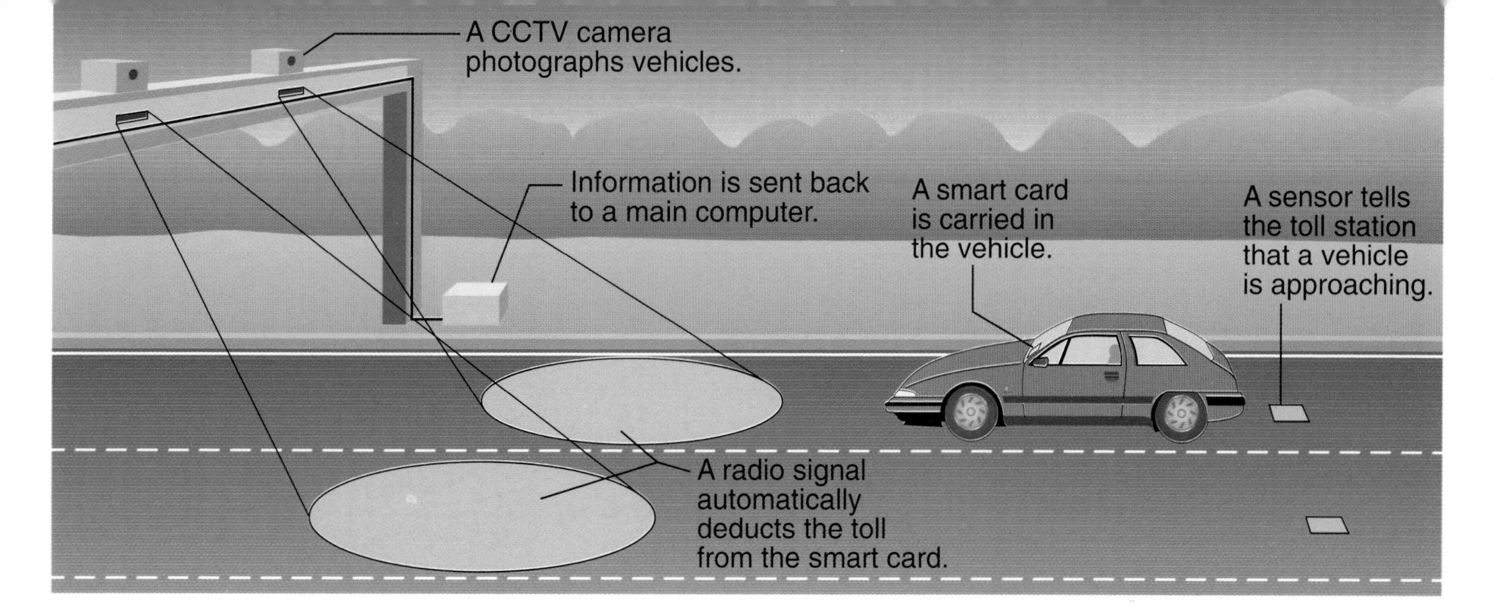

Digital technology means drivers can pay road tolls automatically.

Road tolls

In many countries, motorists pay a toll for using major roads and bridges. Stopping to pay tolls can cause traffic delays, although digital technology already means that drivers do not have to stop at a tollbooth to pay cash. They will be able to pay electronically by buying a smart card. As the car passes a section of tolled road, electronic units are automatically deducted by a roadside receiver.

Car security

The car of the future. On the steering wheel, a route map is displayed, while the dashboard display gives details such as journey time and fuel consumption.

Many cars are now fitted with electronic alarm systems. A microchip embedded in the car's plastic key guard will switch the alarm system on or off as the car is locked or unlocked. Some car keys also work by remote control. A microwave beam locks or unlocks the car, switching the alarm system on or off.

Another security device is the electronic tag. A tiny microchip and aerial hidden on the car acts as a transmitter, enabling the car to be tracked by a satellite, which beams back the position of the car wherever it is, even if it has been stolen and hidden inside a garage.

NAVIGATION

An in-car navigation system. Information on traffic flow is fed into the car's computer, which calculates the best route to avoid delays.

Have you ever been in a car when the driver has been lost? Some cars, like the newest BMWs, are now able to give the driver directions, thanks to an on-board computer.

A small display screen on the dashboard shows the driver a computerized road map with a flashing light indicating the car's position. An arrow shows the correct direction to take. But even more useful is the voice synthesizer, which gives the driver detailed verbal instructions such as "There is a traffic circle coming up in half a mile. When you reach it, make the third right."

If a driver gets lost or finds the road ahead blocked by traffic, the computer will plot a new route.

Satellite tracking

With a technology called global positioning system (GPS), a car can be tracked, using satellite signals. If the car has a receiver, it can tune to the signals transmitted by one of 24 satellites orbiting the earth. By locking onto signals from four satellites, the car's on-board computer can calculate its position.

However, the satellite receiver only gives an accuracy to the nearest 160 ft. (50 m), so the computer compares the GPS information with the distance, speed, and direction in which the car has traveled. And it overlays this information on a map generated by CD-ROM to correct its position.

The computer holds a CD-ROM containing all the road maps for an entire country. A company named Navigation Technologies of California is producing digital maps for the United States and for every country in Europe. Because the task of compiling map data is huge, only major cities have been mapped so far.

There are new developments ahead. Once the maps are in place, other information can be added, such as the details and prices of the main hotels and the locations of garages. Using a mobile telephone, the driver could phone ahead to make a hotel or restaurant reservation. There is even one car computer system that will send a distress call to the nearest garage if the car breaks down.

A driver checks her location with a handheld satellite navigation receiver. The device plots the car's position, using signals beamed from a network of GPS satellites.

A DIGITAL FUTURE

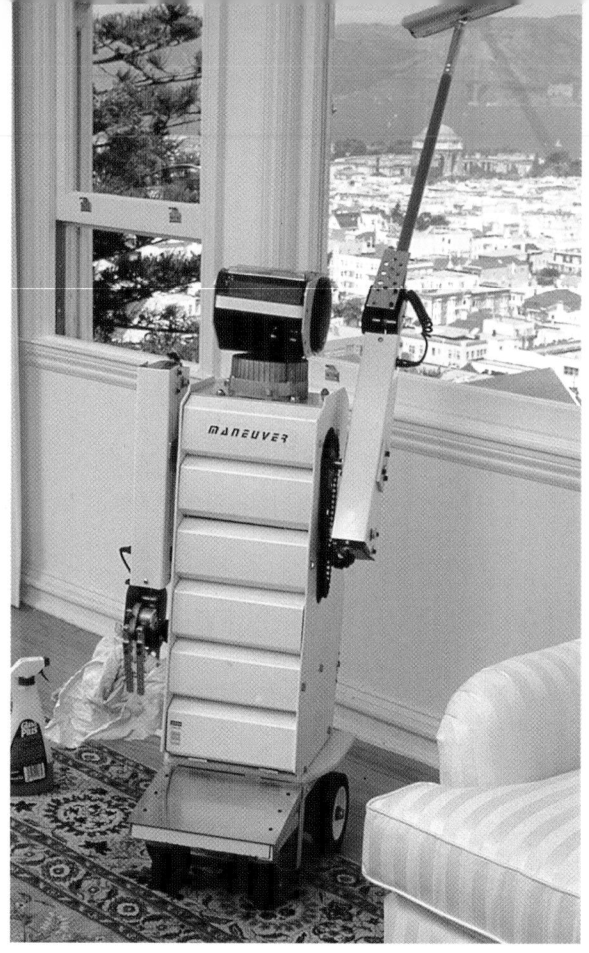

In the future, domestic robots like this could be doing many simple household tasks.

The pace of the digital revolution is so rapid that changes are happening all the time. Different technologies are coming together. Because of this, there will one day be a single, multipurpose machine that can perform the function of a computer, telephone, television, stereo, and multimedia player.

Robots

One day, perhaps we will have programmable domestic robots that can help with the housework. Robots have already been developed that can perform simple tasks like carrying packages. In both the United States and Great Britain, robots are used in some hospitals, helping to deliver meals, mail, or medicine.

Talking computers

Computers can simulate speech, using combinations of electronic sounds. But in the future, as computers become more powerful, they may be able to recognize speech and carry out tasks on a verbal command. They might also be able to recognize handwriting.

An expert working experimental computer software that can recognize human voice patterns. Perhaps one day we will be able to talk to our computers and program them to respond to our verbal commands.

A suspended image system (SIS) television produces a 3-D image that "floats" in the air.

Television

Very large, flat-screen, wall-mounted televisions will have full digital picture quality and stereo sound. Television and interactive services will become "multiplatform." This means that viewers will be able to choose whether the television channel they watch has been transmitted by satellite, by cable, or by conventional broadcasting.

In the future, digital pictures sent by cable or satellite will be unscrambled by a built-in computer inside the television set, instead of the present set-top box. These new televisions will be able to perform all the functions of present-day computers. The Fujitsu and ICL companies have already made a PCTV (personal computer television) that changes from one to the other at the touch of a button.

Today's plastic bank cards contain microchips that enable them to perform a wide range of functions.

A cashless future

Today, people who want to withdraw money from their bank account often go to an automated teller machine (ATM). They insert a special bank card, key in their PIN and the amount they want, and the machine dispenses the money.

Banking technology of the future means that soon you will not need to carry cash and loose change. You will have an electronic "purse"—a plastic card little bigger than a present-day bank card, on which will be stored information about your bank account. You will be able to use the card to pay for goods. It will also be able to store other information so that you will no longer need things like travel tickets, address books, and diaries. No one will be able to steal your money because your card will be programmed to respond only to your voice.

VIRTUAL REALITY

Virtual reality (VR) was first used by the U.S. space agency NASA, to show astronauts what it would be like in space. Using a powerful computer, graphics, video, and stereo sound, a computer could simulate space so well that it looked almost real—hence, the name "virtual." A NASA scientist created a special headset containing two separate miniature televisions to allow the wearer to see the computer-generated images.

As PCs have become increasingly powerful, virtual reality has been developed to allow people to practice other skills such as performing medical operations or learning to fly airplanes. VR can also be used to play interactive computer games. The player usually wears a special headset and controls the game by using a specialized hand control, or "glove."

Wearing virtual reality headgear, a NASA scientist finds out what it would be like to pick up a rock from the surface of Mars.

In the future, people working from home will be able to meet and talk with colleagues based anywhere in the world in a virtual conference. Feeding video telephone links into a computer, 3-D images of people as they speak can be placed around a table and seen on a VR headset. Documents handed out at the meeting can be stored on the computer.

People will be able to take part in VR activities such as football games or visits to "virtual art galleries," where they can meet other people taking part in the same VR simulation.

Communicating in the future

Telephones of the future will incorporate tiny digital video cameras and a television screen so that you can see who you are speaking to. Perhaps VR simulations will, one day, allow people to have a videoconference where they can meet and sit down with the people they are talking to by using 3-D VR headsets.

Videophones enable people to see each other while they talk on the telephone.

DATE CHART

1959 Texas Instruments etches a circuit on a silicon chip.

1969 ARPANET—the forerunner of the Internet—is developed by the U.S. Defense Department.

1970 The first virtual reality flight simulators are developed by General Electric for NASA.

1971 Intel's 4004 microchip becomes the world's first microprocessor.

1976 The Apple II becomes the world's first widely available home computer.

1978 Japanese company Taito Corporation introduces the video computer game Space Invaders, which launches electronic video games.

1979 The first CD for audio recording is launched jointly by Philips and Sony.

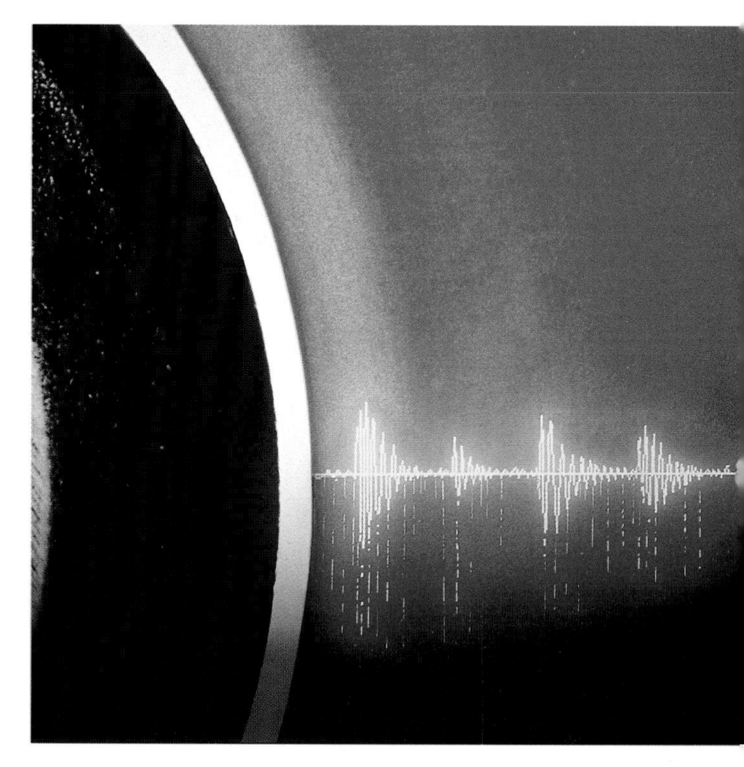

1981 The IBM PC is launched, using Microsoft software.

1985 The CD-ROM is invented by Philips and developed jointly with Sony.

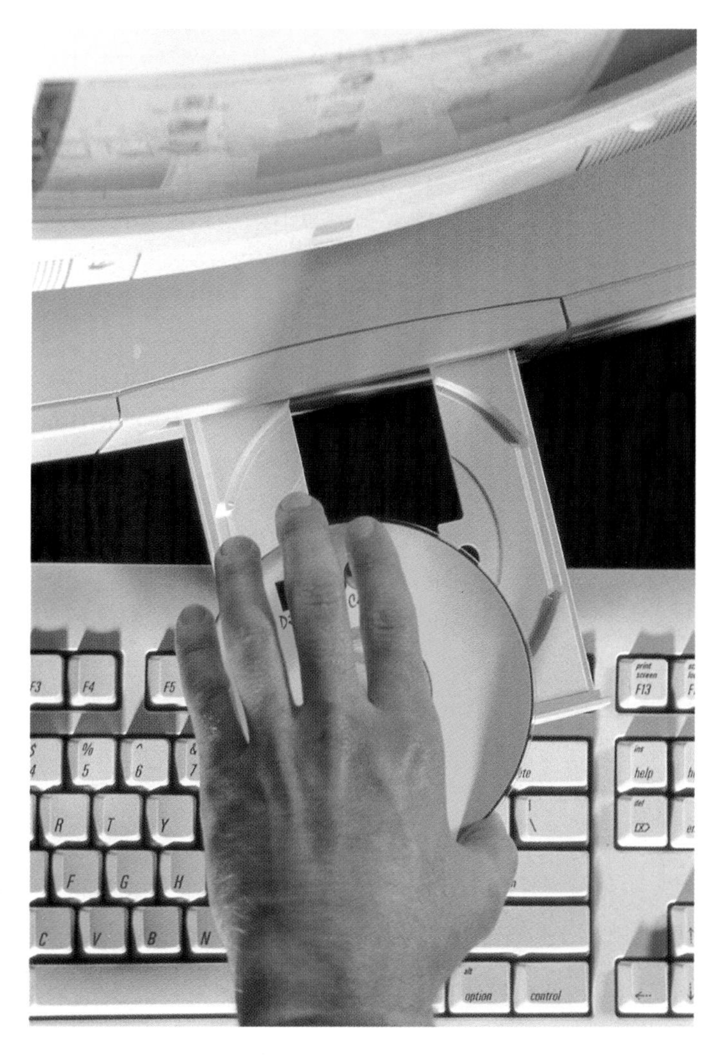

1987 Sony and Philips launch the digital videodisc.

1987 Two separate digital audiotape systems are developed by JVC and Sony.

1989 Nintendo launches its Game Boy machine, a small portable game computer.

1989 Sony begins working on the first recordable CD.

1989 The Japanese company JVC brings out the CD-Midi to produce synthesized music.

1991 The first program is developed to enable people to access the World Wide Web.

1992 Kodak and Philips launch photo-CDs, a system for storing photographs digitally on a CD.

GLOSSARY

animation Moving pictures created by using drawings.
bit A single binary digit—the smallest unit of computer data.
broadband Communications systems that are able to transmit digital information.
cable A system using cables to transmit telephone data, computer data, or television signals.
CCTV (closed-circuit television) Television images transmitted by wires to a receiver. Unlike ordinary television broadcasts, the images are usually sent to a limited number of receivers, for a special purpose, such as security, rather than for entertainment.
CD-ROM (Compact Disc Read Only Memory) A compact disc that carries computer data.
digital Information that is in binary code.
digital exchange A center where digital telephone connections are made.
download To transfer data or computer programs from one computer to another.
electronic mail (E-mail) Messages that are sent from one computer to another via telephone lines.
etched Scratched or marked onto a surface.
facsimiles Electronic transmissions of exact copies of documents.
fiberoptic cable Cables made from thin glass fibers, which are capable of carrying information in the form of pulses of light.
frequency The number of wave peaks that pass a given point each second.
gigabyte One thousand million bytes (groups of eight binary digits).
graphics Data displayed by a computer in the form of a picture.
integrated circuit A silicon chip.
interactive Allowing a two-way flow of information between a computer and the user.
laser A powerful beam of pure light that can travel long distances.
microchip A small piece of material (such as silicon) that is capable of carrying integrated circuits.
microwave An electro-magnetic wave.
multimedia Using many different ways of commun-icating—sound, still and moving images, text, etc.
output Played, used, or displayed via a computer, television, or other electronic device.
personal computers (PCs) Computers that are small enough and cheap enough to be bought for home use.
remote control Controlled at a distance by signals transmitted from a radio or electronic device.
rhythm boxes Electronic machines that produce rhythmic musical sounds.
satellite An object that orbits the earth. Communication satellites receive signals such as telephone or television broadcasts and transmit them to receivers on Earth.
scanner A device for scanning, reading, or examining something.
sensors Devices that can detect and recognize different things, such as light, sound, or electric current.
software Programs that control the operations performed by a computer.
solar panels Panels that trap and use the heat of the sun.
spreadsheets Computer programs for creating and using calculations with numbers.

subscribers People who pay to receive a product or service.
synthesizers An electronic instrument that produces musical sounds.
transistors Devices that control the flow of pulses of electricity. Computer transistors were replaced by the silicon chip.
virtual reality (VR) Simulation of the real world by computer.
voice synthesizer A device that is capable of imitating the human voice.
World Wide Web A network of pages on the Internet that allow people to access and share information easily.

BOOKS TO READ

Bridgman, Roger. *Electronics* (Eyewitness Science). New York: Dorling Kindersley, 1993.

Gardner, Robert. *Communications* (Yesterday's Science, Today's Technology). New York: 21st Century Books, 1994.

Leon, George D. *Electronics Projects for Young Scientists* (Projects for Young Scientists). Danbury, CT: Franklin Watts, 1991.

Locke, Ian. *The Chip and How It Changed the World* (History and Invention). New York: Facts on File, 1995.

Morris, Ting. *Communication* (Craft Topics). Danbury, CT: Franklin Watts, 1996.

Snedden, Robert. *The Internet* (20th Century Inventions). Austin, TX: Raintree Steck-Vaughn, 1997.

Weiss, Anne E. *Virtual Reality: A Door to Cyberspace.* New York: 21st Century Books, 1996.

INDEX

Numbers in **bold** refer to illustrations